A Journey Through Meditation and Verse

Hatty Jones

Published by Hatty Jones, 2024.

While every precaution has been taken in the preparation of this book, the publisher assumes no responsibility for errors or omissions, or for damages resulting from the use of the information contained herein.

A JOURNEY THROUGH MEDITATION AND VERSE

First edition. November 9, 2024.

Copyright © 2024 Hatty Jones.

ISBN: 979-8227990082

Written by Hatty Jones.

A Journey Through Meditation and Verse

A book combining mindfulness practices with poetry to encourage introspection and calm.

In a world that often pulls us in countless directions, where the hum of daily life can drown out the whisper of our inner selves, there is a quiet refuge waiting for us—mindfulness. This book, Poetry for the Mindful: A Journey Through Meditation and Verse, is an invitation to pause, breathe, and step into that sacred space where the mind meets the heart.

Mindfulness is more than a practice; it is a way of being—a gentle return to the present moment, a compassionate embrace of what is. Through these pages, we will explore mindfulness not just as a concept but as a lived experience, using the timeless art of poetry to guide our journey.

Poetry and mindfulness share a common thread: they both invite us to slow down and notice. A poem captures a fleeting moment, a hidden truth, or a tender feeling in words. Similarly, mindfulness teaches us to honour each breath, each sensation, and each thought with curiosity and kindness. Together, they create a harmonious path toward introspection, calm, and connection.

This collection is divided into four sections, each inspired by a facet of mindfulness practice—grounding in the present, cultivating inner awareness, deepening our connection with the world, and embracing acceptance and release. Each poem is an offering, a seed to plant in the fertile soil of your mindfulness journey.

Let these verses be a companion to your practice, a mirror to reflect your inner world, and a bridge to connect with the beauty and complexity of life. You may wish to read them during moments of stillness, at the end of a meditation, or whenever you seek inspiration and calm.

This book is not just for seasoned meditators or poetry enthusiasts—it is for anyone yearning to find peace in a hurried world, anyone searching for the sacred in the ordinary. Together, let us journey through words and awareness, weaving a tapestry of mindfulness and meaning.

May this collection serve as a reminder: peace is always within reach, and mindfulness begins with a single moment of presence.

Welcome to the journey.

Section 1: Grounding in the Present

The Stillness Beneath: Finding Silence Amidst Chaos

In the whirlwind of modern life, where responsibilities pile up like waves crashing against the shore, finding silence and calm often feels unattainable. Our minds race to keep up with the demands of daily existence, and our breaths become shallow, reflecting the tension we carry within. Yet, even amidst the chaos, there lies an opportunity—a profound stillness that waits beneath the surface, like the tranquil depths of the ocean beneath stormy waters. This stillness is accessible to all of us, and it begins with a simple yet powerful tool: the breath.

The Breath as an Anchor

Breathing is a constant companion, a rhythm of life so automatic that we often overlook its significance. Yet, the breath is more than a physiological process; it is a bridge between the body and the mind, a thread connecting the inner and outer worlds. When life feels overwhelming, anchoring yourself in the present moment through mindful breathing can be transformative.

Unlike external circumstances, the breath is always within your control. While you cannot command the chaos of the world to subside, you can direct your focus inward, using the breath as a steady anchor in the storm. By consciously engaging with your breathing, you create space to pause, reflect, and ground yourself in the here and now.

The Practice of Mindful Breathing

Mindful breathing involves paying deliberate attention to your breath without trying to change it. It is a practice of observation, not manipulation—a way to connect with your natural rhythm and bring awareness to the present moment. Here are some breathing exercises that can help you find stillness amidst chaos:

1. The Deep Belly Breath (Diaphragmatic Breathing)

This foundational breathing exercise helps ground you by engaging the diaphragm, allowing you to breathe deeply and fully. It calms the nervous system, reduces stress, and promotes relaxation.

How to Practice:
Find a comfortable seated or lying position.
Place one hand on your chest and the other on your belly.
Inhale deeply through your nose, allowing your belly to rise as your lungs fill with air.
Exhale slowly through your mouth, feeling your belly fall.
Focus on the movement of your belly, letting each breath flow naturally.
As you practice, notice the sensation of the air entering and leaving your body. With each breath, feel yourself grounding more deeply into the present moment, letting go of distractions.

2. The 4-7-8 Breath
This breathing pattern is designed to soothe the mind and body, making it especially effective for finding calm during stressful moments.

How to Practice:
Sit comfortably with your back straight.
Inhale through your nose for a count of 4.
Hold your breath for a count of 7.
Exhale slowly and completely through your mouth for a count of 8.
Repeat the cycle 4-8 times, or until you feel more centered.
This exercise works by elongating the exhale, which activates the parasympathetic nervous system—the body's "rest and digest" mode. It's a simple yet potent way to return to stillness.

3. Box Breathing (Square Breathing)
This technique involves an equal count for each part of the breath cycle, creating a sense of balance and symmetry.

How to Practice:
Inhale through your nose for a count of 4.

Hold your breath for a count of 4.
Exhale through your mouth for a count of 4.
Hold your breath again for a count of 4.
Repeat for several cycles, visualizing a square as you move through each phase.

Box breathing is particularly grounding because it provides structure and rhythm, helping you regain control in moments of chaos.

4. The 2:1 Exhale-to-Inhale Ratio

Extending your exhalation relative to your inhalation has a calming effect on the nervous system. This exercise is ideal when you feel overwhelmed and need immediate grounding.

How to Practice:
Inhale deeply through your nose for a count of 3.
Exhale slowly through your mouth for a count of 6.
Continue this pattern, adjusting the counts as needed to maintain a 2:1 ratio.

Focus on the sensation of release during the exhale, imagining your stress and tension leaving your body with each breath.

Finding Silence Amidst Chaos

Breathing exercises are not just tools for relaxation; they are gateways to a deeper awareness of the present moment. By focusing on your breath, you cultivate mindfulness—the practice of being fully present with whatever arises, without judgment. This presence is the essence of grounding, allowing you to access the stillness beneath the surface.

When chaos surrounds you, mindful breathing provides a way to pause and step back. It reminds you that while you cannot control external events, you can choose how you respond. With each conscious breath, you reaffirm your connection to the here and now, anchoring yourself in the steady rhythm of life.

Integrating Breathing Exercises into Daily Life

The beauty of breathing exercises is their accessibility. You don't need special equipment, a dedicated space, or a large block of time. They can be practiced anytime, anywhere—at your desk, in the car, or during a moment of solitude.

Here are some tips for integrating mindful breathing into your daily routine:

Morning Practice: Begin your day with 5-10 minutes of deep belly breathing to set a calm and focused tone.

Midday Pause: Use a technique like box breathing to reset during a busy workday or stressful moment.

Evening Wind-Down: Practice the 4-7-8 breath before bed to release the tension of the day and prepare for restful sleep.

On-the-Go Moments: Whenever you feel overwhelmed, take a few deep breaths, using any technique that resonates with you.

The key is consistency. The more you practice, the more natural it becomes to turn to your breath for grounding and calm.

The Transformative Power of Stillness

As you engage with your breath, you may notice subtle shifts—a quieting of the mind, a softening of tension in the body, a sense of spaciousness within. These moments of stillness are not the absence of chaos but a reorientation to it. They are an acknowledgment that beneath the surface of our busy lives, there is a wellspring of peace waiting to be tapped.

Finding stillness does not mean escaping the realities of life; it means meeting them with greater clarity and resilience. Through mindful breathing, you cultivate the capacity to stay present amidst challenges, to approach life's storms with a calm and grounded spirit.

A Journey Within

In the practice of mindful breathing, you embark on a journey within—a journey to discover the stillness that has always been there, beneath the noise and distractions. This stillness is not something you need to create; it is your natural state, uncovered through the gentle act of paying attention.

As you continue to explore the breath, you may find that it becomes more than a grounding tool; it becomes a teacher. The breath teaches patience, reminding you that calm cannot be rushed. It teaches acceptance, showing you how to flow with life rather than resist it. And it teaches gratitude, as each breath is a gift, a reminder of the vitality and beauty of being alive.

In the chaos of the world, finding silence may feel like an impossible task. Yet, the stillness you seek is always within you, accessible through the simple, profound act of breathing. By anchoring yourself in the present moment, you discover a refuge that no storm can shake—a place of peace, resilience, and grounding. This is the gift of mindful breathing: a path to the stillness beneath.

The Breath Between

Inhale deeply, the chaos fades,
Exhale slowly, stillness pervades.
The hum of life, a distant drone,
In breath's rhythm, you're not alone.
The mind, a tempest, thoughts collide,
Yet breath's soft pulse becomes your guide.
A harbour calm amidst the storm,
A sacred pause where peace takes form.
Feel the air, so cool, so warm,
Its steady flow, the silent norm.
Each breath a step, the present calls,
Through stillness vast, the chaos falls.
Anchor yourself in this embrace,
The breath, your refuge, endless space.

Roots of the Earth

Feet planted firm on sacred ground,
The earth beneath, the pulse profound.
A world spins wild, yet here you stand,
Held by the quiet strength of land.
Feel the soil, its steady hum,
The chaos wanes, the peace will come.
Close your eyes, let senses drift,
The earth below, a grounding gift.
The trees above, their roots so deep,
Teach you where your soul may keep.
In stillness vast, where roots entwine,
Find that steady ground as thine.
You are the earth, the earth is you,
In stillness found, the moment true.

Whisper of the Wind

The wind whispers, soft and low,
A gentle guide for where to go.
It bends the trees, it sways the leaves,
Yet softly still, it soothes and weaves.
In chaos loud, it finds a song,
A breath that carries life along.
Feel its touch upon your skin,
Its endless journey deep within.
The world may roar, the winds still flow,
A quiet peace you'll come to know.
Close your eyes, and let it teach,
The calm of winds is in your reach.
In every breeze, in every gust,
Find stillness waiting, learn to trust.

Pebbles in the Stream

A stream flows onward, swift and clear,
Its gentle song dissolves your fear.
Pebbles rest upon its bed,
Unmoved by waters overhead.
The chaos rushes, wild and free,
Yet pebbles stay in harmony.
Be like the stone, steadfast and still,
Let waters pass; bend to their will.
Feel the stream wash through your mind,
A cleansing path, a peace to find.
Each drop, a thought, that comes and goes,
Each ripple fades, no turmoil shows.
Be still, be calm, like pebbles wait,
For chaos flows, and peace is fate.

The Eye of the Storm

A tempest rages all around,
Yet in its heart, no sound is found.
The eye, a space of purest calm,
A fleeting pause, a healing balm.
Life's storms may twist, their winds may howl,
Yet silence waits amidst the growl.
Step to the center, breathe and see,
The chaos fades, and you are free.
The stillness vast, it holds no fear,
For in its space, the truth is clear.
A moment's peace, a sacred vow,
No storm can break the present now.
Find the eye, and there remain,
Through breath, the calm you will regain.

Sky Beyond the Clouds

The clouds may gather, dark and vast,
Yet skies beyond are clear, steadfast.
The storm will pass, its fury spent,
The heavens wait, their calm unbent.
Your thoughts may swirl, your mind may race,
Yet stillness lives in boundless space.
Close your eyes, look past the storm,
Feel the quiet skies take form.
A single breath dissolves the haze,
A gentle light begins to blaze.
The present moment, vast and free,
The sky beyond is where you'll be.
Chaos wanes, the silence calls,
Beyond the clouds, no shadow falls.

The Quiet Flame

The flame flickers, soft and bright,
A steady glow in endless night.
The wind may blow, the shadows loom,
Yet still it burns, defies the gloom.
Chaos tries to snuff it out,
To fill the space with fear and doubt.
Yet deep within, the flame remains,
A quiet force through life's refrains.
Focus now, let breath sustain,
The inner light that will remain.
It does not waver, does not flee,
The stillness burns eternally.
In chaos fierce, this truth is plain:
Your light within will still remain.

Mountain's Heart

The mountain stands, both fierce and still,
A timeless strength, an endless will.
The winds may rage, the rains may fall,
Yet mountains rise, unyielding, tall.
Be like the peak, unmoved, secure,
A grounded calm, a peace so pure.
Inhale deeply, feel its stone,
Exhale slowly, claim your throne.
The chaos fades, the mind will clear,
The mountain's heart will draw you near.
No storm can break the grounded soul,
No wind can shift its steady goal.
Be like the mountain, strong and wise,
The stillness deep beneath the skies.

Echoes of Silence

In the cavern, echoes play,
Repeating what we fear to say.
Yet listen close, and you will find,
The quiet hum that soothes the mind.
The chaos loud may call your name,
Yet silence answers all the same.
A breath, a pause, a gentle sigh,
The echoes fade, the fears will die.
Let stillness fill the empty space,
A sacred calm, a healing grace.
The noise dissolves, the quiet grows,
The inner peace that always knows.
Amidst the echoes, find your way,
To silence vast where stillness stays.

The Pulse of Life

Beneath the noise, a steady beat,
The pulse of life is calm, discreet.
The heart, it whispers, soft and true,
A rhythm constant, guiding you.
The chaos shouts, the moments flee,
Yet here's a pulse, eternally.
Feel it rise with every breath,
A silent vow that conquers death.
In stillness deep, the pulse will guide,
A truth within where peace resides.
Return to it when storms arise,
Its gentle strength will never lie.
The pulse of life is always near,
A grounding force to calm your fear.

Breath of Life

Inhale softly, the world draws near,
Exhale gently, dissolve your fear.
A simple act, yet vast in scope,
Each breath a thread, each breath a hope.
The breath connects, it softly ties,
The earth below, the endless skies.
A rhythm ancient, strong and deep,
A cradle calm where thoughts can sleep.
The air flows in, the body learns,
The air flows out, the balance turns.
No need to grasp, no need to hold,
The breath will guide, its story told.
With every breath, life speaks to you,
A truth so simple, yet always true.

The Ocean of Air

The breath, an ocean, deep and wide,
Its gentle waves forever glide.
Each inhale swells, a tide that grows,
Each exhale falls, the current flows.
The chaos fades with every crest,
The rhythm holds, it knows what's best.
A sailor lost, you find your way,
The breath, your compass, leads each day.
Close your eyes, feel its embrace,
Its boundless calm, its steady pace.
Through every storm, through every gale,
The breath, your anchor, will prevail.
An ocean vast, a timeless guide,
The breath connects, no need to hide.

Bridge to the Now

The breath, a bridge from there to here,
It spans the gap, it draws you near.
Each moment held, each moment flows,
The breath, a guide the body knows.
Step onto this sacred span,
Its gentle rhythm holds the plan.
A present pause, a mindful rest,
A quiet space where life feels blessed.
No future fears, no past remains,
The breath dissolves your inner chains.
Its whispers soft, its pulse so true,
Connects the world to inner you.
The bridge endures, its path is clear,
The breath will lead, no need to steer.

Breath as a Teacher

The breath, a teacher, kind and wise,
It shows the truth beyond the lies.
No need to rush, no need to strive,
The breath reminds you: you're alive.
Each inhale speaks of what you need,
Each exhale whispers: let it bleed.
The worries leave, the peace remains,
The breath removes what brings you pain.
No words it needs, no lessons loud,
It teaches soft amidst the crowd.
Its message simple, ever clear:
The present moment's always here.
Learn from the breath, its patient ways,
And let its wisdom fill your days.

A Gentle Companion

The breath, a friend who walks beside,
A constant guide through life's rough tide.
Its whisper low, its presence near,
A source of calm when doubt appears.
No matter where your journey goes,
The breath remains, it softly flows.
Through joy or pain, through dark or light,
It stays with you, a faithful might.
Feel its rhythm, trust its care,
It carries you through thin and rare.
Each breath a step, each step is sure,
The breath provides, its path secure.
A gentle friend, so wise and true,
The breath will always stay with you.

The Dance of the Breath

The breath, a dancer, sways with grace,
It flows through time, it finds its space.
Each inhale lifts, a gentle rise,
Each exhale falls, where stillness lies.
A rhythm constant, soft, and true,
A sacred dance within and through.
Feel its steps, its silent beat,
The breath, a partner, pure and sweet.
Through life's chaos, it does not stray,
The breath will guide you through the fray.
No need to lead, just follow near,
Its steady pace will calm your fear.
The breath, a dance that never ends,
A rhythm deep that life defends.

Threads of the Breath

The breath, a thread that weaves the whole,
It ties together heart and soul.
A single thread, yet endless spun,
It links the many, joins the one.
Each breath you take connects you more,
To earth below, to sky, to shore.
Its subtle weave, its gentle line,
It binds your life, a thread divine.
Through every breath, the world aligns,
Its whisper blends with nature's signs.
Feel the thread, its strength, its grace,
The breath connects all time and space.
A tapestry of life it weaves,
Through breath, the universe achieves.

Breathing the Moment

The moment comes, the moment goes,
The breath, a witness, softly shows.
It does not cling, it does not flee,
It simply is, it lets you be.
Through every rise, through every fall,
The breath remains, it holds it all.
A fleeting now, yet vast, complete,
Through every breath, the present meets.
Inhale deeply, the world arrives,
Exhale softly, the moment thrives.
Feel its rhythm, its ebb, its flow,
The breath will teach all you must know.
No moment lost, no future near,
The breath reveals the now is here.

The Infinite Breath

The breath, a cycle without end,
It moves through time, it does not bend.
A circle drawn in sacred air,
A timeless loop, beyond compare.
Each breath begins, then fades away,
Yet never lost, it stays in play.
A symbol vast, of life's refrain,
The breath returns, and starts again.
Feel its flow, eternal, free,
A rhythm vast as any sea.
It joins the past, the future too,
Through every breath, the infinite true.
Inhale softly, exhale clear,
The breath connects all far and near.

The Song of the Breath

The breath, a song with notes so light,
It sings of peace through day and night.
No words it needs, its melody,
Resounds within, a symphony.
Each inhale hums a quiet tone,
Each exhale deep, a chord alone.
Together bound, the notes align,
A song of life, a truth divine.
Listen closely, feel its sound,
The breath, a song where peace is found.
Its music holds, its rhythm stays,
A hymn that guides through all your days.
The breath, a song both soft and strong,
It carries you, where you belong.

Rooted Balance

Beneath my feet, the roots descend,
Into the soil, where journeys blend.
Each tendril seeks the earth's embrace,
A grounding force, a sacred space.
Above, the branches stretch to skies,
Their leaves like whispers, soft replies.
Between the worlds, I stand in grace,
A bridge of life, a timeless place.
The roots hold firm, the branches sway,
Both earth and sky shape my array.
I am the tree, both strong and free,
In balance lies my destiny.
Grounded deep, yet reaching high,
I claim my place beneath the sky.

The Earth's Whisper

The soil whispers, calm and deep,
A promise made, a vow to keep.
The roots entwine, they hold, they bind,
A sacred tether, strong yet kind.
The sky responds, a call to soar,
To reach beyond, to seek for more.
Between these forces, here I stand,
With earth below, and sky at hand.
Feel the strength of grounded care,
The freedom in the open air.
Both forces pull, yet both unite,
The tree within, a guiding light.
Rooted firmly, reaching wide,
In nature's arms, I do reside.

Bridge of Life

A tree stands tall, its roots dig deep,
A balance wrought in nature's keep.
Its branches arch toward the sun,
Its leaves a song of lives begun.
The earth supports, it holds, sustains,
Through drought, through storm, through gentle rains.
The sky inspires, it calls to grow,
To stretch toward dreams we may not know.
Between the two, the balance lies,
A harmony that never dies.
We, like the tree, must find our way,
To stand as bridges, come what may.
Both rooted firm and reaching far,
Guided by earth, and every star.

The Dance of Roots and Sky

Roots embrace the earth's deep core,
A steady pulse, a quiet shore.
They twist and twine in darkened earth,
A hidden strength that knows its worth.
The branches sway in skies above,
A dance of freedom, hope, and love.
They seek the sun, they touch the breeze,
They thrive in endless mysteries.
The tree unites what seems apart,
Its roots the ground, its leaves the heart.
It teaches us to bridge the two,
To anchor firm and still pursue.
The earth below, the sky above,
A tree's embrace of life and love.

Silent Connection

Feet on the soil, arms to the sky,
I feel the world as moments fly.
The earth is calm, its whispers low,
The sky responds with breezes slow.
The roots entwine, they cradle deep,
A promise strong, a bond to keep.
The branches wave in endless play,
A gentle reach, a bright ballet.
We, too, are trees in life's grand scheme,
Rooted strong, yet free to dream.
Our grounding gives the strength to rise,
Our dreams unfold in endless skies.
In nature's rhythm, find your place,
A union bound by time and space.

The Tree Within

Inside us all, the tree resides,
Its roots, its branches, its vast divides.
It teaches balance, calm, and grace,
To root in soil, yet seek wide space.
Its roots remind us where we're from,
The soil that shapes, the roots we hum.
The branches stretch to futures bright,
Aiming always toward the light.
We are the tree, both strong and kind,
With roots that ground, with dreams aligned.
In every breath, we feel its sway,
Its timeless pull, its guiding way.
Rooted firmly, we still aspire,
The earth our base, the sky our fire.

Bound by Earth and Sky

The soil cradles, the sky inspires,
A tree's deep roots, its lofty spires.
The balance found within its frame,
A life of stillness, growth, and flame.
The roots go down, they find their place,
They weave in soil, a sacred space.
The branches reach, they touch the air,
In search of light, of dreams, of care.
Between the two, the trunk resides,
A steady core where life abides.
It knows its role, it plays its part,
Rooted body, dreaming heart.
To live as trees is what we seek,
Firm and grounded, strong yet meek.

Roots Below, Sky Above

The roots, they burrow, dark and low,
Through earth's embrace, where life does flow.
A stable base, a grounded start,
A home for tree, a home for heart.
The sky above, it calls with light,
A beckoning to reach new height.
The branches sway, they twist, they climb,
A dance eternal, defying time.
Together joined, these forces blend,
A tree's true purpose knows no end.
Its roots and leaves, a mirrored grace,
Both earth and sky, its dwelling place.
We, too, must learn from nature's plan,
To root, to rise, to simply stand.

The Stream Within

A stream flows softly, cool and clear,
Its whispers soothe the things we fear.
The pebbles fall, they sink, they rest,
The stream moves onward, ever blessed.
Each thought a pebble, sharp or round,
Its edges smoothed as it is drowned.
The waters take what we release,
And offer back a sense of peace.
The stream flows on, it doesn't cling,
To any stone or fleeting thing.
Let worries drop, let thoughts drift by,
And feel the calm beneath the sky.
The stream within will guide the way,
Through letting go, the fears decay.

Carried Away

A pebble drops into the stream,
A ripple born, a fleeting gleam.
The water swirls, then flows anew,
The pebble rests in depths of blue.
Our worries fall like stones unseen,
Disturbing briefly, but serene.
Release them all, let go the weight,
The current pulls, it knows the state.
The stream is vast, it carries care,
Its endless flow dissolves despair.
Each worry sinks, each thought takes flight,
The waters soothe, they heal, they right.
Trust in the stream, it knows the way,
To wash the heavy fears away.

The River Knows

The river knows no need to hold,
Its waters young, its waters old.
Each stone it takes, it does not keep,
It simply flows, both wide and deep.
Let worries fall like stones you bear,
Release their weight into the air.
The current takes them, one by one,
And softens edges sharp as sun.
Your thoughts, like pebbles, find their place,
Beneath the stream, a calm embrace.
No need to grasp, no need to fight,
The water moves, it makes things right.
The river knows, it always will,
Through letting go, your heart grows still.

Pebbles of the Mind

Each thought a pebble, smooth or rough,
A burden light, a burden tough.
It clutters streams with weight and fear,
Yet waters wait to draw them near.
Drop the stone, release the grip,
Let it sink with quiet slip.
The stream will take it, find its bed,
And calm the chatter in your head.
For every thought, a place is found,
Beneath the waters, safe and sound.
The stream flows onward, clear and true,
It washes all that troubles you.
Be still, let go, and watch them fade,
The pebbles rest, your peace is made.

The Weightless Stream

The stream flows light, its song so pure,
A balm for worries to endure.
Each pebble tossed, it sinks below,
The current takes it where it'll go.
Release the weight, let burdens slide,
The stream will hold them, deep inside.
No stone too sharp, no load too vast,
The stream will smooth them all at last.
Its waters endless, strong, and kind,
They cradle thoughts that cloud your mind.
Feel the freedom, light as air,
The stream absorbs your every care.
Flow with the stream, and let it show,
The peace that comes from letting go.

Ripples Fade

A thought arises, sharp and bright,
A pebble tossed in morning light.
It splashes down, the ripples spread,
Then silence calms the water's bed.
The ripples fade, the surface clears,
No trace remains of fleeting fears.
The stream remembers not the fall,
It flows beyond, it welcomes all.
So cast your worries, let them sink,
No need to hold, no need to think.
The stream will take what's not your own,
And leave you light, your burdens flown.
Each pebble tossed, a step to peace,
In letting go, your cares release.

Rest Beneath the Flow

The stream flows constant, strong and true,
Its waters bright, its depths askew.
A pebble drops, it finds its way,
Beneath the flow, it learns to stay.
Each worry thrown becomes the stone,
Yet in the stream, it's not alone.
The waters cradle, soothe, and mend,
They offer peace, a journey's end.
Release the thought, no need to clutch,
The stream provides a healing touch.
Its flow unending, vast, and free,
It carries all to where they'll be.
Rest beneath the flow, let go,
The stream will teach what you must know.

The Silent Depths

The stream runs silent, calm, and clear,
It holds no grudge, it keeps no fear.
The pebbles sink to depths below,
The current whispers, "Let them go."
Each worry falls, it finds its place,
A quiet bed, a soft embrace.
No ripples last, no marks remain,
The stream dissolves what brings us pain.
Trust the waters, let them guide,
And feel the peace they hold inside.
The silent depths, so vast and wide,
Will cradle all the fears you hide.
Through every thought, through every care,
The stream flows on, and you repair.

Section 2: Inner Awareness

Echoes Within: Listening to the Quiet Voice of the Self

In the hustle of daily life, where distractions beckon from every corner, it is easy to lose touch with our inner selves. We are pulled outward by the demands of others, the hum of technology, and the constant need to be productive. Yet beneath this cacophony lies a quiet space—a sanctuary within where the true self resides. It is in this space that we can hear the gentle "echoes within," the whispers of intuition and self-awareness that guide us to understanding, balance, and peace.

The journey to inner awareness begins with listening—not just to the world around us, but to the subtleties of our inner voice. This requires mindfulness, patience, and an openness to explore parts of ourselves we might not always acknowledge. By cultivating this self-awareness, we create a foundation for living with authenticity and clarity, even amidst the noise of the outside world.

The Noise and the Quiet

Modern life often feels like a relentless stream of external input. Notifications buzz, conversations demand attention, and our own thoughts seem to race in competition with the world. This external noise can drown out the subtler voice of our inner self, making it difficult to discern what we truly feel, need, or believe.

But the voice within is always there, even if faint. It manifests in moments of stillness—a fleeting sense of calm, a gut feeling, or an inexplicable clarity about what truly matters. Listening to this voice requires us to create space, to quiet the external and internal chatter, and to tune into the resonance of our inner echoes.

The Practice of Inner Listening

Tuning into the echoes within is not about achieving absolute silence or suppressing thoughts. Rather, it is about observing and gently peeling back the layers of noise to hear what lies beneath. Here are a few steps to help you connect with your inner awareness:

Create Stillness: Find a quiet space where you can sit comfortably without distractions. This need not be elaborate—a simple corner where you feel safe and undisturbed is enough.

Focus on Breath: Begin by focusing on your breath, using its natural rhythm as an anchor. The steady inhale and exhale can help calm the mind and create a sense of presence.

Notice Without Judgment: Allow thoughts to arise without trying to push them away or analyse them. Instead, imagine each thought as a ripple on the surface of a pond—acknowledge it, and let it pass.

Ask Open Questions: Gently ask yourself open-ended questions like, "What do I truly need right now?" or "What is my inner voice telling me?" Then, listen without expectation or urgency.

Embrace the Pause: Sometimes the echoes within are quiet, offering no immediate answers. Embrace the pause and trust that clarity will emerge with time.

Recognizing the Echoes

Inner awareness often comes in subtle forms—an intuitive nudge, a feeling of discomfort or joy, or a persistent thought that keeps resurfacing. Recognizing these signals is the first step toward understanding them. Here are a few ways the echoes within might present themselves:

Physical Sensations: Tightness in the chest, a flutter in the stomach, or a deep sense of relaxation can indicate emotional responses. Listening to your body can reveal truths your mind has yet to articulate.

Emotional Patterns: Notice recurring emotions, such as frustration, gratitude, or fear. These patterns often point to underlying needs or values.

Intuitive Clarity: Sometimes, without logical explanation, you "just know" something is right or wrong for you. Trusting these moments can guide you toward greater alignment with your true self.

The Power of Inner Awareness

Developing inner awareness offers profound benefits. It strengthens your ability to make decisions that align with your values, enhances emotional resilience, and fosters a deeper sense of connection with yourself and others. By tuning into the echoes within, you learn to distinguish between the noise of the world and the truths of your heart.

This self-awareness also empowers you to navigate life's challenges with grace. When you are grounded in your inner truth, external turbulence becomes less overwhelming. You can respond to situations with clarity and intention, rather than reacting from a place of confusion or fear.

Practical Tools for Cultivating Inner Awareness

1. Mindful Journaling

Writing is a powerful way to access the inner voice. Set aside time each day to journal freely about your thoughts, feelings, and experiences. Ask yourself reflective questions, such as:

"What emotions am I carrying today?"

"What does my body feel right now, and what might it be telling me?"

"What is something I truly desire or fear?"

Journaling allows your inner voice to come forth unfiltered, offering insights you may not consciously realize.

2. Meditation Practices

Meditation is a cornerstone of listening to the echoes within. Guided meditations focused on inner awareness can help you connect with your true self. Visualization techniques, such as imagining a calm lake reflecting your thoughts, can also foster a sense of inner clarity.

3. Body Scans

A body scan involves bringing attention to each part of your body, starting from the toes and moving upward. This practice helps you notice sensations or tension that might hold emotional or mental clues.

4. Nature Connection

Spending time in nature can quiet the mind and enhance self-awareness. Walk barefoot on the earth, listen to the rustling of leaves, or simply sit under a tree. Nature's calm provides a mirror to reflect the peace within.

5. Self-Affirmations

Affirmations are a direct way to align with your inner voice. Repeating positive statements helps you cultivate trust in yourself and strengthen your connection to your deeper truths.

Five Affirmations for Inner Awareness:

I trust my inner voice to guide me with clarity and wisdom.

I am present and open to listening to my true self.

In stillness, I find the answers I seek.

My emotions and sensations are valuable teachers.

I am connected to my inner wisdom and act with intention.

Repeat these affirmations daily, especially during moments of quiet reflection, to reinforce your inner awareness.

Overcoming Barriers to Inner Awareness

While the practice of tuning into the echoes within is deeply rewarding, it is not always easy. The noise of self-doubt, external pressures, or fear of confronting difficult emotions can create barriers. Recognizing these obstacles is the first step to moving past them.

1. Fear of What You Might Discover

Sometimes, we avoid inner listening because we fear confronting uncomfortable truths. Remember, self-awareness is not about judgment—it is about understanding. What you discover within is part of your journey and an opportunity for growth.

2. Overwhelming Noise

The world's demands can make it difficult to find the time or space to listen inward. Prioritize moments of stillness, even if brief. A single deep breath or a five-minute pause can make a difference.

3. Impatience

Inner awareness unfolds gradually. Trust the process and let go of the need for immediate clarity. The echoes within may whisper softly, but with patience, their message will become clear.

The Journey to Your True Self

Listening to the echoes within is a lifelong practice. It is not about perfection or achieving a final destination—it is about cultivating a relationship with yourself. Each moment of awareness brings you closer to your true self, allowing you to live with greater authenticity and peace.

When you honour the quiet voice inside, you align with your inner truth. This alignment brings a sense of freedom, as you no longer feel the need to conform to external expectations or suppress your emotions. You become empowered to act from a place of self-awareness, guided by the wisdom within.

The Resonance of Inner Peace

As you deepen your practice of inner awareness, you may notice a resonance—a sense of harmony that arises when you are in tune with yourself. This resonance is the true gift of listening to the echoes within. It is a reminder that, no matter how noisy the world becomes, you carry within you a sanctuary of peace and wisdom.

Return to this sanctuary often. Nurture it with moments of stillness, mindful practices, and affirmations that reinforce your connection to yourself. With time, the echoes within will become a steady guide, helping you navigate life's complexities with grace and clarity.

You are your own best teacher. Your inner voice holds the answers you seek. Trust it, nurture it, and let it lead you home.

The Whispering Soul

Amidst the chaos, soft and low,
A voice within begins to grow.
It whispers truths the world can't see,
A quiet call to simply be.
No shouts, no cries, no loud demand,
Just gentle guidance, hand in hand.
It waits in stillness, calm and clear,
A presence strong, yet full of care.
The world may pull, its noise may swell,
But inner whispers softly tell:
"You are enough, no need to race,
Find peace within, a sacred space."
Listen close, the voice is wise,
It shows the self, where freedom lies.

The Quiet Compass

The world distracts with constant din,
Yet truth resides somewhere within.
A compass clear, it always knows,
Which way to turn, the path that shows.
Its needle points with steadfast grace,
A guiding star, a quiet space.
No clamour shakes its steady beat,
It leads you home, where life feels sweet.
Close your eyes, the noise will fade,
The inner guide comes to your aid.
Its wisdom whispers, soft and near,
A voice to trust, a voice sincere.
Through storms and doubt, it points the way,
Your inner truth will never sway.

Echoes of Peace

The echoes call, they gently sound,
Through depths where quiet truths are found.
They ripple soft, through thought and mind,
A soothing balm, a peace aligned.
The outside world may clamour loud,
Its fleeting noise a restless shroud.
Yet echoes linger, pure and true,
They offer calm to cradle you.
Feel their rhythm, their quiet flow,
A sacred space where wisdom grows.
They speak of strength, of love, of worth,
They tether you to grounded earth.
In every breath, the echoes sing,
A melody to which you cling.

Beyond the Noise

The world is loud, its pull severe,
It clouds the truths we hold so dear.
Yet underneath, a voice is clear,
It calls us back, it draws us near.
Through layers thick of doubt and fear,
It whispers truths we long to hear.
No need to shout, no need to fight,
The quiet voice reveals the light.
Turn from the noise, the rush, the glare,
And seek the voice that's always there.
Its song is still, its tone is wise,
It lifts you up where silence lies.
Beyond the noise, your self remains,
Its quiet strength through all sustains.

The Voice of Truth

A voice within, a timeless sound,
Its wisdom waits where calm is found.
It does not clamour, boast, or plead,
But softly speaks to every need.
It holds no grudge, it casts no blame,
It seeks no power, seeks no fame.
It simply is, a steady guide,
A beacon strong you hold inside.
Through every trial, every pain,
The voice remains, its truths sustain.
Lean in, be still, and you will hear,
Its gentle words dissolve your fear.
This voice of truth, so pure, so kind,
Leads you back to peace of mind.

Silent Echoes

The echoes drift through silent air,
A voice that whispers, "I am there."
No need to search, no need to roam,
The self-resides, its quiet home.
It hums a tune both soft and sweet,
A steady rhythm, calm and complete.
Its notes arise when all is still,
A song that soothes, a guiding will.
The noise recedes, the world takes pause,
The echoes sing without applause.
In every note, a truth revealed,
A hidden strength, a wound that's healed.
The echoes tell what words can't say,
To guide you gently on your way.

A Mirror Untouched

The self reflects in waters calm,
A mirror still, a soothing balm.
No ripples mar, no noise distorts,
A truth unshaken, clear reports.
This mirror speaks without a sound,
Its quiet depths profound, unbound.
Look closely, see the self-anew,
A silent voice that guides you through.
No clamour here, no need to strive,
The self is steady, pure, alive.
Beneath the noise, beyond the fray,
Its quiet truths will light the way.
This mirror waits, it always will,
A voice of calm when all is still.

The Depths Within

Dive deep beneath the rushing waves,
Where silence dwells in hidden caves.
The echoes linger, soft and clear,
A map of truths both far and near.
No storm can shake the depths you hold,
A quiet realm, serene and bold.
Its currents steady, its waters pure,
A reservoir of strength, secure.
The noise above may rage and roar,
But here within, there's always more.
A voice that echoes calm and grace,
A sanctuary, a sacred space.
Dive deep, explore, and you will find,
The quiet strength within your mind.

The Listener's Gift

The world may speak in hurried tone,
Its rush can leave you all alone.
But pause, be still, and you will see,
The quiet self will set you free.
To listen is a gift so rare,
It clears the fog, it lifts despair.
The voice within, though soft and shy,
Reveals the truths that cannot lie.
Lean in, receive its sacred song,
Its wisdom steady, pure, and strong.
It speaks of love, of strength, of peace,
Of letting go, of sweet release.
The listener hears, the self-aligns,
A quiet voice, where calm combines.

The Echo's Call

A call resounds, so soft, so faint,
It holds no boast, it wears no paint.
Its power lies in quiet tones,
A voice that leads you to your own.
No need to chase, no need to force,
The echo waits, its steady course.
Through stillness found, through silence made,
The echo calls, its truths conveyed.
It tells of worth, of peace, of trust,
A voice that guides with wisdom just.
Beyond the noise, its whispers flow,
A truth the heart has always known.
The echo calls, its sound is clear,
A voice within to hold you near.

The Untouched Mirror

A mirror waits, so calm, so still,
Reflecting truth without a will.
It shows the self, no mask, no guise,
A pure reflection, honest eyes.
No judgment lingers in its frame,
No fault to seek, no need for blame.
It sees you whole, it sees you true,
A gentle gaze that welcomes you.
Look deep within, what do you see?
A being vast, a mystery.
The flaws dissolve, the doubts take flight,
The mirror glows with inner light.
Accept the truth, embrace your face,
The mirror shows your boundless grace.

A Compassionate View

The mirror whispers, soft and kind,
"No need to fear what you will find."
It shows your heart, it shows your pain,
Yet through it all, you still remain.
Each line, each scar, each tender trace,
Is part of you, your sacred space.
No flaw too deep, no wound too wide,
The mirror sees with love, not pride.
Be gentle now, let kindness flow,
The mirror wants for you to know:
Your worth is vast, your soul complete,
No need to hide, no need to cheat.
Embrace the view, release the strife,
The mirror loves your precious life.

Beyond the Surface

A mirror holds what eyes can't see,
A deeper truth, a mystery.
Beneath the skin, beyond the face,
A story dwells in every space.
It doesn't judge, it doesn't blame,
It doesn't play the ego's game.
Instead, it offers clarity,
A glimpse of your complexity.
Look deeper still, the mirror waits,
To show you love that never hates.
Accept the truth, the flaws, the light,
For all are part of endless might.
In this reflection, free from lies,
Your truest self begins to rise.

Reflections of Love

The mirror gleams, a surface bright,
It captures all, in dark and light.
But what it shows is up to you,
Will you judge or see it true?
Release the need to criticize,
To find the faults in weary eyes.
Instead, look closer, see with care,
The love that's always hidden there.
Each line a story, each mark a song,
A journey winding, hard and long.
The mirror speaks with soft embrace,
It shows the beauty in your face.
No perfect form, no flawless skin,
Just perfect love that lies within.

Through Kind Eyes

The mirror stands, a quiet friend,
A guide to where your truths extend.
It doesn't filter, twist, or frame,
It doesn't scold, it doesn't shame.
Instead, it offers something rare,
A view of you, beyond compare.
But only if you dare to see,
The self you are, unconditionally.
Be kind to what the mirror shows,
For even pain and doubt bestows,
A lesson learned, a wisdom gained,
A self that rises, unrestrained.
Through kindest eyes, the mirror's glow,
Reflects the love you need to know.

The Truth Beneath

A mirror stands without a veil,
It doesn't falter, doesn't fail.
It shows the truth, the full display,
No need to look the other way.
But truth is not a weapon sharp,
It's not the critic's cutting harp.
It's soft, it's kind, it's full of grace,
It's what you need to face your face.
See what's beneath the surface glare,
The heart that beats, the love that's there.
A soul that's fought, a soul that's won,
A soul that's strong, though battles run.
The truth beneath will set you free,
The mirror shows who you must be.

A Gentle Reflection

The mirror whispers, "Come and see,
The one you are, who longs to be."
It doesn't mock, it doesn't pry,
It doesn't ask the reason why.
It shows you scars, it shows you tears,
But also strength through all your years.
It shows the joy, the laughter bright,
The moments pure, the love, the light.
Let go of judgment, breathe and stare,
See yourself with tender care.
No need to change, no need to hide,
The mirror stands forever by your side.
Its love is steady, soft, and true,
The mirror simply shows all you.

Light Within the Frame

A mirror frames the world you know,
Reflects the self, the seeds you sow.
But deeper still, beyond the glass,
Lies truths that time and fear surpass.
It shows your glow, your inner fire,
Your boundless dreams, your soul's desire.
No shadow dims, no flaw can break,
The light within that mirrors take.
Let judgment fade, let kindness grow,
Allow the self its strength to show.
The light within is yours to keep,
A flame that burns in waters deep.
See your reflection, soft and clear,
The mirror holds all you hold dear.

The Mirror's Gift

A mirror gives, it does not take,
A gift of truth, a path to make.
It shows your past, it shows your now,
It whispers, "Trust yourself somehow."
Its gift is not in what it sees,
But how it asks your heart to ease.
No need for doubt, no room for shame,
It shows the self without a name.
A mirror's gift is love unbound,
A grace in which all worth is found.
Accept this gift, this quiet call,
To love the self, to love it all.
Its gift is you, just as you are,
A shining soul, a constant star.

Free of Judgment

The mirror waits, serene and pure,
Its purpose steady, safe, secure.
It doesn't point, it doesn't blame,
It doesn't tarnish with a name.
It simply shows what you must see,
The self-that's vast, the self-that's free.
No labels here, no standards high,
Just you beneath the open sky.
Take in this view, this gift of grace,
Your tender soul, your shining face.
Release the weight of judgment's call,
The mirror holds no weight at all.
Free of bias, pure and true,
It shows the beauty born in you.

The Lantern's Flame

A lantern glows through shadowed night,
Its warmth persists, a steady light.
Though darkness creeps and doubts take hold,
The lantern burns, its flame is bold.
No storm can snuff its quiet gleam,
No fear can quench its endless dream.
It holds within a boundless peace,
A soft, unyielding, sweet release.
When times are hard, its glow remains,
A beacon strong through life's terrains.
So guard the flame, its light is true,
It burns within, a part of you.
Through every trial, let it shine,
Your inner light, your strength divine.

The Keeper's Trust

In moments dark, the keeper stands,
A lantern bright within their hands.
Its glow may falter, dim, or sway,
Yet never does it fade away.
For deep inside, its flame endures,
A quiet strength that gently cures.
The keeper trusts its steady glow,
No matter what the winds may blow.
Through storms of doubt, through tides of fear,
The lantern holds the keeper near.
Its light a promise, calm and wise,
A guiding star through shadowed skies.
Trust in the flame, for it will show,
The path ahead, the way to go.

A Light That Lasts

The lantern shines, though winds may howl,
Its flame defies the shadows' scowl.
A fragile spark, yet strong, it stays,
A beacon through the darkest days.
The light it casts is soft and warm,
A refuge in the fiercest storm.
It does not waver, does not flee,
It burns for you, eternally.
Hold fast this light, it will not fail,
Its glow remains through life's travail.
For in its fire, your strength resides,
A force that through the darkness guides.
No night too long, no fear too deep,
The lantern's light is yours to keep.

The Inner Glow

Within your heart, a lantern rests,
Its glow the answer to life's tests.
No outer storm can take its flame,
No doubt can strip it of its name.
Its light is born of love and care,
A spark of hope beyond compare.
Through every trial, through every fall,
The lantern rises, guiding all.
It whispers truths the soul can hear,
A melody of strength and cheer.
Protect this glow, let it inspire,
A flame that burns, a sacred fire.
For when the world feels cold and grim,
The lantern glows, its light within.

Through the Darkness

The night may fall, the winds may rise,
Yet still the lantern never dies.
Its flame persists, its warmth remains,
A constant through the shifting plains.
When shadows press and doubts encroach,
The lantern shines with calm reproach.
Its light a bridge, a steady stream,
A gentle glow, a quiet beam.
Hold to its flame when all seems lost,
It burns despite the bitter frost.
For in the dark, it finds its place,
A beacon lit by inner grace.
Through trials harsh, through sorrow's sting,
The lantern keeps your soul's bright spring.

The Keeper's Light

The keeper holds a lantern clear,
Its glow a shield from doubt and fear.
It lights the way when paths are blind,
A guide the heart can always find.
Though winds may rage and rains may pour,
Its steadfast flame shines evermore.
The keeper knows it's worth is vast,
A light to steer, a truth to last.
When voices shout and shadows fall,
The lantern answers, guiding all.
Its flame reflects the soul's true peace,
A quiet glow that cannot cease.
In every storm, through every fight,
The keeper guards this sacred light.

A Flame Unbroken

The flame endures through thick and thin,
A quiet strength that burns within.
It flickers not when shadows loom,
But fills the space with gentle bloom.
Though life may toss and turn the tide,
The lantern's light will always guide.
It does not falter, fade, or stray,
It stands through night to greet the day.
This flame is yours, it does not flee,
A fire of calm resiliency.
Protect its glow, let it expand,
It rests secure within your hand.
For when the dark seems all you know,
The lantern lights the way to go.

The Eternal Spark

The spark ignites, a glowing thread,
A lantern lit, its warmth widespread.
It stays through sorrow, holds through strife,
A quiet fire sustaining life.
The keeper guards it, pure and true,
Its light a gift to guide them through.
No gale can quench, no rain can drown,
This flame that wears no fear nor frown.
When all seems lost, the lantern stays,
Its glow a hymn, its light a praise.
It whispers softly, "I am here,
A constant guide, a calm, sincere."
In every heart, this spark abides,
A lantern flame that never hides.

Passing Shadows

The clouds may gather, dark and low,
But winds will come, and they will go.
No storm can last, no shadow stay,
The sky will clear, the light will play.
So let the clouds drift where they might,
Through day and dusk, through silent night.
The self remains, the soul serene,
Beneath the clouds, the sky is clean.
Accept the storm, and let it be.

The Open Sky

The sky above is vast and blue,
It holds no grudge, it stays in view.
Though clouds may darken, storms may cry,
The endless sky will never die.
Each thought a cloud, it floats away,
No need to grasp, no need to stay.
Beneath the noise, the self is clear,
A space of calm, forever near.
The sky remains, the storm departs.

Drifting Wisps

The clouds arrive, their forms take shape,
But soon they shift, they can't escape.
They may seem strong, their shadows wide,
Yet light persists on every side.
The thoughts that press are just the same,
They come and go, without a name.
Accept their presence, let them pass,
Like fleeting wisps through skies of glass.
Your peace resides beyond their reach.

Winds of Change

The winds will blow, the clouds will drift,
Their shapes may frighten, dark and swift.
Yet time will pull their edges thin,
And skies will open bright again.
The mind is vast, a boundless sea,
Its storms are brief, its calm is free.
Embrace the clouds, their fleeting stay,
For all will pass, they fade away.
Your steady core remains unchanged.

The Clearing Light

A heavy cloud may cross your sight,
Yet soon it fades into the light.
No thought can linger, harsh or kind,
The sky is larger than the mind.
Accept the rain, the storm, the grey,
They too are part of every day.
But know the truth, the constant glow:
Above the clouds, your peace will grow.
The light remains; it always shines.

Section 3: Celebrating Simplicity

The Touch of Morning Dew: Celebrating Simplicity and the Beauty of Small Moments

In the rush of life, it is easy to overlook the beauty that surrounds us. The world's demands often blind us to the gifts that exist in the simplicity of small moments—the touch of morning dew on grass, the gentle warmth of sunlight on the skin, or the rhythmic sound of rain tapping against a window. These seemingly ordinary experiences are extraordinary when approached with mindful observation. They anchor us in the present moment and connect us to the larger world with a sense of gratitude, peace, and wonder.

The Gift of Small Moments

Life is a collection of fleeting moments. Often, we focus on the grand milestones and miss the quiet, everyday joys that give life its texture and depth. The simplicity of a cool breeze, the scent of flowers in bloom, or the first sip of morning coffee are all invitations to slow down and be fully present.

The beauty of small moments lies in their ability to ground us. When we pause to notice the world around us, we engage all our senses. This act of mindful observation transforms ordinary moments into extraordinary ones, enriching our lives with connection and meaning.

The Practice of Mindful Observation

Mindful observation is the art of paying attention—fully and without judgment—to the world around you. It requires no special tools or training, just the willingness to slow down and notice. Here are some suggestions for cultivating this practice:

Start with Your Senses: Use your senses to engage with the present moment. What do you see, hear, smell, taste, or feel? Let each sensation draw you into the now.

Example: Feel the softness of the morning dew underfoot or the warmth of a sunbeam on your face.

Be Present with Curiosity: Approach each moment with a beginner's mind, as if you are experiencing it for the first time. Notice the details you might otherwise overlook.

Example: Observe how light filters through leaves or the intricate patterns on a seashell.

Pause and Breathe: Take a moment to stop whatever you're doing and simply breathe. Let your breath anchor you to the present moment, making it easier to notice the small joys around you.

Practice Gratitude: Acknowledge and appreciate the beauty in the simple things you encounter. Gratitude enhances your sense of connection to the world.

The Beauty of Morning Dew

Morning dew is a perfect metaphor for the fleeting beauty of small moments. Its tiny droplets catch the light and glisten like jewels, yet they vanish as the day warms. Dew is delicate and impermanent, reminding us that life's beauty often lies in its transience.

When we pause to feel the coolness of dew on our fingertips or watch how it sparkles on blades of grass, we connect with a profound sense of presence. This connection grounds us in the now, fostering inner calm and a deeper appreciation for life's subtle wonders.

Mantra: "I honour the beauty in each moment, knowing it is precious and unique."

Mantras and Affirmations for Connection

Mantras and affirmations can deepen your practice of mindful observation and help cultivate a sense of connection with the world. Repeat them silently or aloud during moments of stillness or while engaging with nature.

Mantras:
"With each breath, I see the beauty around me."
"I open my heart to the simplicity of life's moments."

"The world's wonders unfold when I am fully present."
Affirmations:
I am connected to the beauty of the world through my senses.
I find joy in life's small, simple moments.
Every moment offers a gift of wonder and peace.
I slow down to appreciate the richness of the present.
The beauty of the world reminds me of my own inner calm.
Suggestions for Embracing Simplicity
Create Rituals Around Small Moments: Turn everyday activities into rituals of mindfulness. For example, when you drink your morning tea or coffee, focus on the aroma, warmth, and taste rather than rushing through the experience.

Spend Time in Nature: Nature has a way of revealing life's quiet beauty. Take walks, sit by a stream, or watch the clouds. Observe how nature thrives in its simplicity.

Practice Gratitude Journaling: Each day, write down three small things you appreciated. This practice trains your mind to notice and savour the little joys in life.

Be Present with Loved Ones: Notice the small gestures of kindness and connection in your relationships. A smile, a laugh, or a gentle touch can deepen your sense of connection with others.

Limit Distractions: Put away your phone or other distractions for a few minutes each day to allow space for mindful observation.

The Transformative Power of Small Moments

Mindfully observing small moments can transform your relationship with the world. It shifts your focus from what is lacking to what is abundant, from future worries to present joys. This practice fosters a sense of gratitude and contentment, helping you navigate life with greater resilience and peace.

Affirmation: "I am open to the beauty and abundance that surrounds me every day."

Over time, this habit of mindful observation becomes second nature. You start noticing the little things that bring joy—a child's laughter, the sound of birdsong, or the colors of a sunset. These small moments weave into the fabric of your day, enriching your life in ways that are both profound and lasting.

Journaling Prompts for Mindful Observation

Journaling is a powerful way to deepen your practice of celebrating simplicity. Use these prompts to reflect on your experiences:

What small moments brought you joy today?

Describe a time when you felt fully present. What did you notice?

How did engaging with nature affect your mood or perspective?

Write about a sensory experience (sight, sound, touch, taste, or smell) that stood out to you recently.

What are three simple things you are grateful for today?

Embracing the Present

Life is fleeting, like morning dew evaporating under the sun. Yet, it is in these fleeting moments that we find the richness of existence. By grounding ourselves in the simplicity of sensations and observing the beauty in everyday life, we cultivate a deeper connection to the world and to ourselves.

When you honour the touch of morning dew, the rustle of leaves, or the softness of a breeze, you are not just noticing the world—you are participating in it. These moments remind us that we are not separate from nature or life but deeply intertwined with it.

Mantra: "I am one with the world, connected by its beauty and rhythm."

The Power of Awareness

Mindful observation teaches us a profound truth: the small things are not small at all. They are the building blocks of our lives, the moments that shape our memories and enrich our souls.

The next time you step outside, pause and look around. Notice the light on the trees, the scent of earth, or the sound of distant laughter. Let these moments anchor you in the present and remind you of the beauty that surrounds you, even in the simplest of things.

Affirmation: "The beauty of life is in the present moment, and I embrace it fully."

A Closing Reflection

The touch of morning dew symbolizes life's ephemeral nature and its endless beauty. By practicing mindful observation, we open ourselves to the wonder of small moments and the deep connection they foster. This practice doesn't require dramatic changes or grand gestures—just a willingness to slow down, notice, and appreciate.

Carry these words with you:

Simplicity is sacred.

Beauty is everywhere, waiting to be seen.

The world speaks to those who listen.

With mindful observation, you can transform your life, one simple moment at a time.

The Tapestry of Life

Beneath the stars, a web is spun,
Connecting all, both moon and sun.
A thread of light, a golden weave,
A truth unseen, yet we believe.
Each life a strand, both strong and thin,
Entwined without, entwined within.
No thread alone, no strand apart,
Together woven, heart to heart.
The tapestry grows with every breath,
It binds the living, even death.
Each being joined in sacred art,
A masterpiece where all take part.
The threads connect, the fabric glows,
In every soul, the infinite shows.

Invisible Bonds

The threads are silent, yet they bind,
A woven truth for heart and mind.
From earth to sky, from birth to death,
They hold the rhythm of our breath.
One thread begins where others start,
A web of life, a single heart.
Through joy and grief, through fear and love,
These threads are gifts from realms above.
You touch the world, it touches you,
Each act, each thought, a thread anew.
Invisible, yet always there,
A bond we carry everywhere.
The threads remind: we're not alone,
Each life a strand the cosmos owns.

Web of Being

A spider spins its fragile thread,
Between the branches, overhead.
The web reflects the morning dew,
A vision vast, profound, and true.
So too, our lives are finely spun,
Each thread connected, everyone.
We share the space, the air, the ground,
Our spirits linked where none are bound.
The web extends through time and space,
Uniting all, the human race.
No single life can stand apart,
For threads of love entwine the heart.
A fragile web, yet ever strong,
The threads of being carry on.

The Golden Thread

The thread of gold runs through the night,
A subtle glow, a guiding light.
It ties the stars, it binds the seas,
It whispers truths on every breeze.
No thread alone completes the weave,
Each life a strand, each heart a sleeve.
Together formed, a boundless whole,
A cosmic quilt of every soul.
The golden thread runs through us all,
From mighty peaks to shadows small.
It tells us we are not apart,
But woven close, heart into heart.
So cherish each, both near and far,
For every thread is who we are.

The Loom of Life

Upon the loom, the threads align,
Each stitch, each weave, a love divine.
The colors blend, the patterns grow,
A boundless beauty starts to show.
The loom is vast, it has no end,
Its threads of life forever bend.
Each being adds a vibrant hue,
A story told, a path renewed.
The fabric holds, though stretched and worn,
By trials faced, by dreams reborn.
It tells of hope, of pain and cheer,
A woven tale that draws us near.
The loom of life connects us all,
Through every thread, we rise or fall.

Threads Unseen

The threads we walk, we cannot see,
Yet they unite both you and me.
Through every glance, through every deed,
These threads fulfil a deeper need.
A single thread may seem so small,
But it connects us, one and all.
Through words exchanged, through hearts that care,
These threads remind us, we are there.
They cross the oceans, span the skies,
They bridge the gaps where silence lies.
Invisible, yet strong and true,
These threads hold fast, connecting you.
In every life, a thread will be,
A part of one great tapestry.

The Infinite Web

The infinite web extends its reach,
A silent lesson life can teach.
Each thread a path, a soul, a bond,
Connecting worlds both here and beyond.
The web reflects the morning's glow,
A mirrored truth we come to know.
That every being, large or small,
Belongs within the web of all.
Its strands hold firm through time's great test,
Each thread a chance to do our best.
For when we pull, the web responds,
It answers back with sacred bonds.
The infinite web surrounds us whole,
It binds each heart, it feeds each soul.

Threads of Light

The threads of light stretch far and wide,
They hold the stars, they touch the tide.
They weave through moments, time, and space,
A glowing net of boundless grace.
Each life a spark within this net,
A thread that ties, a path that's set.
No thread alone can ever shine,
Together formed, they make design.
These threads of light unite our hearts,
They mend the wounds, they heal the parts.
A luminous, eternal string,
Connecting every living thing.
Feel the threads, they're always near,
A light to guide, a bond to cheer.

Eternal Bonds

Between the stars, the threads are spun,
A sacred weave that holds each one.
Through space they stretch, through hearts they flow,
An unseen bond that helps us grow.
Each soul connects, each life entwined,
A bond of spirit, heart, and mind.
These threads of love, they cannot break,
They hold the world for every sake.
When doubts arise, when shadows fall,
The threads remind: we're part of all.
No thread alone can form the whole,
Together they create the soul.
The bonds endure, they never cease,
In every thread, we find our peace.

The Thread Within

Within us all, a thread begins,
A spark of light where love begins.
It reaches out, it stretches far,
Connecting hearts, a guiding star.
This thread connects both friend and foe,
A tie that holds through joy and woe.
Its strength resides in acts of care,
A quiet bond beyond compare.
The thread within, the thread without,
Is forged in trust, dispelling doubt.
For when we love, the thread shines clear,
A bond that grows with every year.
Embrace the thread, it leads the way,
To unity that will not sway.

The Symphony of Light

The sunlight sings a golden tune,
A melody from morn to noon.
Its notes cascade on leaves and stone,
A harmony of worlds unknown.
It warms the earth, it lights the skies,
Its music hums where silence lies.
A quiet rhythm, soft and pure,
A song of life that will endure.
The rays connect both far and near,
A universal hymn we hear.
Through shadowed paths and open plains,
The sunlight's song forever reigns.
Its gentle chords unite us all,
A radiant voice, a timeless call.

The Golden Song

The sun ascends, its tune begins,
A whisper soft, yet deep within.
Its golden notes in waves unfold,
A quiet song, both bright and bold.
Each ray a chord, each gleam a beat,
A symphony both calm and sweet.
It dances through the morning air,
A melody beyond compare.
The earth responds with joyous praise,
As sunlight fills the fleeting haze.
A bond is formed, unseen, yet true,
Between the light, the world, and you.
In every beam, the music flows,
A song of life the sunlight knows.

Light's Eternal Choir

The sunlight sings a choral hymn,
A radiance that won't grow dim.
Its voice ascends on warming air,
A timeless echo everywhere.
Each beam a verse, each glow a phrase,
A sacred tune through endless days.
It touches oceans, mountains, trees,
A melody that rides the breeze.
Its music joins each heart and soul,
A symphony that makes us whole.
No place too vast, no heart too small,
The sunlight sings, connecting all.
Its choir resounds, a voice so near,
Uniting all who choose to hear.

The Radiant Voice

The sun speaks softly through its rays,
Its voice a balm on weary days.
It sings to leaves, to stone, to sea,
A gentle tune of unity.
Each glint reflects a note of cheer,
Its melody both far and near.
It fills the air, it warms the skin,
Its music echoes deep within.
The world responds, it joins the song,
In light's embrace, we all belong.
No boundary breaks the radiant flow,
Its voice connects all life below.
In sunlight's sound, we find our place,
A hymn of light, a world of grace.

The Sunlit Melody

The sunlight hums a gentle tune,
It greets the dawn, it holds the moon.
Its golden chords cascade and rise,
A music born of boundless skies.
It weaves through trees, it lights the streams,
A melody that feeds our dreams.
Its rhythm beats in hearts and stone,
A tune that claims the world its own.
Through every crack, through every shade,
Its song persists, it does not fade.
The sunlight sings for all to hear,
A music pure, profound, sincere.
Its melody unites the earth,
A timeless hymn of life's great worth.

The Glow's Song

The light breaks forth, its voice expands,
It flows through skies, it fills the lands.
Each ray a note, each gleam a sound,
Its symphony is all around.
The fields respond, the rivers sway,
The mountains hum at break of day.
The sunlight's voice a soothing hymn,
It graces all with love within.
It binds the stars, it warms the earth,
A melody of endless worth.
No heart untouched, no soul denied,
The sunlight's song, a sacred guide.
Listen close, its tune is near,
A sound of light, so bright, so clear.

The Sun's Serenade

The sunlight plays a soft refrain,
Its golden notes dissolve the rain.
It dances through the morning dew,
A song of life in every hue.
Its chords resound through fields and trees,
Its melody rides every breeze.
The waves reflect its tender tone,
A serenade of life unknown.
The sun's sweet song unites us all,
Its music answers nature's call.
No voice too quiet, no heart too still,
The sunlight sings; it always will.
In every ray, a verse unfolds,
A song of love the sunlight holds.

The Harmony of Rays

Each ray of sunlight strikes a chord,
A melody the earth adored.
Its music flows through every vein,
A sacred tune that knows no pain.
The flowers bloom, the rivers gleam,
Its harmony fulfils the dream.
Each leaf responds, each shadow sways,
The sunlight hums through endless days.
Its gentle notes connect the skies,
Its chorus lifts, it never dies.
Through every heart, its rhythm moves,
A song of light that life approves.
The harmony of sunlight's sound,
A gift of love, forever found.

The Song Beyond Words

The sunlight sings, it needs no voice,
Its silent song makes hearts rejoice.
Its tune descends with golden glow,
A melody the spirit knows.
Each morning brings its opening chord,
A radiant gift we can't afford.
It binds the world in threads of light,
Uniting all through day and night.
Its music whispers, soft and sweet,
It touches all, it makes life complete.
The song is endless, pure, and bright,
A chorus sung by endless light.
Beyond all words, its tune is clear,
The sunlight sings, it draws us near.

The Everlasting Song

The sunlight's tune is soft and sure,
A music vast, forever pure.
It touches earth, it kisses skies,
A melody that never dies.
Each beam a voice, each glow a key,
Its harmony connects the sea.
The waves respond, the trees agree,
A song of love, of unity.
It echoes through both time and space,
It warms the world with soft embrace.
The sunlight's song, so true, so kind,
A melody for heart and mind.
It binds us all in golden streams,
A song of life, a world of dreams.

The Gift of Gratitude

Hands folded soft, a quiet prayer,
A moment still, a breath of care.
The heart reflects, the soul takes pause,
A simple thanks for life's great cause.
For every joy, for every tear,
For lessons learned through love and fear.
Gratitude shines, its light extends,
It bridges hearts, it mends, it bends.
The act of thanks transforms the way,
We see the night, we greet the day.
With hands folded, peace takes flight,
A heart of thanks ignites the light.

A Heart Reborn

Gratitude blooms in hearts once torn,
A fragile seed, a soul reborn.
It turns the pain, it heals the wound,
A tender song, a sacred tune.
In every breath, in every sigh,
A reason to give thanks draws nigh.
For even storms can cleanse the land,
A blessing waits in every hand.
Fold your palms and close your eyes,
Feel gratitude begin to rise.
Its warmth will cradle, calm, and bind,
Transforming heart, renewing mind.

The Quiet Offering

No grand display, no need for show,
Gratitude's light begins to glow.
A humble act, a whispered plea,
A quiet thanks to what must be.
It holds no grudge, it casts no blame,
It warms the heart, it feeds the flame.
Through trials tough, through moments sweet,
Gratitude lays its gifts at your feet.
Fold your hands and let it flow,
For what you have and what you'll grow.
This simple act will guide you through,
Transforming life with all you do.

The Healing Thanks

Hands clasped in thanks, the soul repairs,
Through whispered thoughts, through humble prayers.
Gratitude heals where scars remain,
It soothes the ache, it mends the pain.
For every loss, for every gain,
The heart grows strong through joy and strain.
No shadow dark can hold its sway,
When gratitude lights up the way.
A folded hand, a grateful heart,
Transforms the whole through every part.
Its power endless, soft, and true,
Gratitude changes all in you.

The Light Within

Gratitude glows, a sacred fire,
It lifts the heart, it draws it higher.
Its warmth transcends the darkest hour,
A gift of grace, a gentle power.
With folded hands, the thanks arise,
A prayer that reaches open skies.
No matter what the day may bring,
Gratitude helps the soul to sing.
It finds the joy in smallest things,
A bird in flight, the song it sings.
Through thanks, the soul becomes complete,
A quiet strength beneath our feet.

The Endless Prayer

Gratitude flows in endless streams,
It lifts the heart, it fuels the dreams.
Through folded hands, the thanks extend,
A prayer to love, a call to mend.
It fills the gaps where sorrow lay,
It lights the dark, it clears the way.
Each moment holds a gift unseen,
A quiet joy, a life serene.
Let gratitude your anchor be,
A constant hymn of harmony.
With every breath, the thanks will grow,
A sacred gift the heart will know.

Section 4: Acceptance and Release

The Dance of Shadows: Embracing Life's Dualities

Life is a dance of contrasts. It moves in rhythms of light and dark, joy and sorrow, hope and despair. These dualities, though seemingly opposites, are not adversaries—they are partners in the dance of existence. By embracing both the light and the shadows, we find balance, growth, and deeper understanding. Acceptance and release become the guiding steps in this eternal dance, helping us navigate the complexities of life with grace and wisdom.

Embracing Duality

Life's dualities are not a sign of imperfection but of wholeness. Without darkness, we would not recognize the brilliance of light; without sorrow, we would not feel the depth of joy. These contrasts shape our experiences, teaching us resilience and compassion. The key to harmony lies not in resisting the shadows but in welcoming them as part of the larger picture.

The dance of shadows is a reminder that all things are fleeting. Just as the sun sets and rises again, joy and sorrow ebb and flow, teaching us to embrace life's impermanence. When we accept both the light and the dark, we open ourselves to the full spectrum of existence.

Mantra: "I embrace life's dualities, knowing they create the wholeness of my being."

The Practice of Acceptance

Acceptance is not passive resignation but an active engagement with reality. It allows us to see things as they are, without resistance or judgment. Through acceptance, we find freedom from the weight of expectation and the pain of denial.

Steps to Practice Acceptance:

Acknowledge What Is: Begin by observing your current experience. Whether it's joy or sorrow, light or shadow, allow yourself to feel it fully without pushing it away or clinging to it.

Release Judgment: Let go of labelling emotions or experiences as "good" or "bad." Instead, view them as natural parts of the human journey.

Breathe into the Present Moment: Use your breath as an anchor to ground yourself. With each inhale, welcome what is; with each exhale, release resistance.

Find the Lesson: Every experience, whether pleasant or painful, holds a lesson. Ask yourself, "What is this moment teaching me?"

Cultivate Gratitude: Even in shadows, there is light. Seek out small moments of gratitude to balance the heaviness of challenging times.

Affirmation: "I accept life as it is, trusting in its rhythm and flow."

The Power of Release

While acceptance allows us to hold space for all that is, release helps us let go of what no longer serves us. Holding onto past pain, regret, or fear creates unnecessary weight. Release is the act of freeing ourselves from these burdens, making space for growth and renewal.

Suggestions for Releasing Emotional Weight:

Journaling: Write down what you are holding onto—whether it's anger, sadness, or regret. Then, visualize releasing these feelings as you close your journal or even tear out the page.

Meditation: Focus on your breath and imagine exhaling what no longer serves you. Each breath out becomes an act of letting go.

Nature Connection: Spend time outdoors and visualize the wind carrying away your worries, or let the water of a stream symbolize the flow of release.

Symbolic Acts: Perform a symbolic gesture, such as lighting a candle for release or placing stones in a stream to represent letting go of burdens.

Mantra: "I release what no longer serves me, making space for peace and renewal."

The Dance of Shadows

The interplay of light and shadow creates life's most profound beauty. Imagine a painting without contrast, or a melody without silence between notes. Just as shadows enhance the brilliance of light, life's challenges deepen our appreciation of its joys.

Mantra: "I dance with both shadow and light, honouring the fullness of life's design."

Here are some ways to honour and embrace life's dualities:

1. Practice Non-Attachment

Avoid clinging to moments of joy or pushing away moments of sorrow. Both are temporary and part of the cycle. By practicing non-attachment, you can move through life with greater ease.

Affirmation: "I flow with life's rhythm, embracing each moment as it comes."

2. Recognize the Growth in Shadows

Shadows often hold the lessons we need most. Reflect on times of challenge and recognize the strength and wisdom you gained.

Suggestion: During moments of difficulty, ask yourself, "What is this experience teaching me?"

3. Celebrate the Light

While shadows teach us, the light replenishes us. Be fully present in moments of joy, gratitude, and peace. Celebrate these moments without fear of their impermanence.

Affirmation: "I celebrate life's light, knowing it nourishes my soul."

4. Balance Action and Rest

Life's dualities also manifest in how we live—between action and rest, giving and receiving. Honor both energies to maintain balance.

Suggestion: Set aside time for intentional rest and reflection, balancing your active pursuits with stillness.

Suggestions for Embracing Balance

Daily Reflection: Spend five minutes each day reflecting on both the joys and challenges you experienced. Acknowledge how both contributed to your growth.

Gratitude and Release Ritual: At the end of each day, write down one thing you are grateful for and one thing you wish to release.

Mindful Movement: Engage in practices like yoga or tai chi, which emphasize the harmony of opposing forces—effort and ease, strength and flexibility.

Nature Walks: Observe the interplay of light and shadow in nature, noticing how they coexist to create beauty.

Intentional Breathing: Practice alternate nostril breathing (Nadi Shodhana) to balance the body and mind, symbolizing the unity of opposites.

Mantra: "I honour both the shadows and the light, finding balance in their dance."

Transformative Power of Balance

When we embrace the dance of shadows, we transform our relationship with life's challenges. Instead of fearing pain or clinging to joy, we learn to appreciate the richness that both bring. This perspective fosters resilience, as we trust in life's cycles and our ability to navigate them.

The practice of acceptance and release helps us stay grounded. By accepting what is, we free ourselves from the struggle against reality. By releasing what no longer serves us, we open ourselves to renewal. Together, these practices create a balanced life—one that honours both the light and the dark.

Affirmation: "I trust in life's cycles, knowing I have the strength to embrace all it brings."

Journaling Prompts for Reflection

What dualities in your life have shaped you most profoundly?
How do moments of light and shadow contribute to your growth?
What is one thing you are holding onto that you could release?
How do you find balance between action and rest, joy and sorrow?
What does embracing life's dualities mean to you?

A Final Reflection

The dance of shadows is life's most exquisite movement. It reminds us that nothing is permanent—neither joy nor sorrow, light nor dark. By accepting this truth, we free ourselves from the fear of change and open our hearts to the beauty of life's impermanence.

This dance is not about choosing one over the other but about moving gracefully between them. It is about trusting that each step, each turn, has its purpose in the choreography of existence.

Mantra: "I find peace in the ebb and flow, knowing each step is part of life's dance."

In the end, it is the interplay of light and shadow that creates the masterpiece of our lives. By embracing both, we honour the fullness of our human experience and connect to the deeper rhythms of the world around us. Through acceptance and release, we learn to dance with life's dualities, finding balance, beauty, and peace.

The Eternal Dance

The shadows shift, the light breaks through,
Each moment holds both old and new.
The dark may fall, the bright may rise,
Yet both are needed in the skies.
For joy and sorrow weave a thread,
A tapestry where both are wed.
Without the night, how would we see,
The gentle glow of dawn's decree?
The dance of shadows moves as one,
Through storms of rain, through golden sun.
Each step in sync, each beat aligned,
A balance deep within the mind.
Embrace the dance, its fleeting sway,
It leads the heart through night and day.

The Shadow's Gift

The shadow comes, it claims its place,
A quiet truth we must embrace.
It softens light, it frames its glow,
A hidden depth we come to know.
For in the dark, the seeds are sown,
A strength that only trials have grown.
The light returns, it shines so bright,
Yet shadows give that glow its height.
Without the dark, there'd be no hue,
No canvas broad for life's review.
So honour both, the dim and gleam,
For each completes the other's dream.
In shadow's gift, a lesson lies,
To seek the light with open eyes.

The Balance Within

The world is neither black nor white,
It lives between, a shifting light.
The shadows stretch, the brightness fades,
Yet both are part of life's charades.
A tear may fall, a laugh may rise,
Each moment blends beneath the skies.
No joy is pure, no grief complete,
They intertwine where hearts do meet.
The balance lives in every part,
It shapes the mind, it fills the heart.
To walk the line, to hold the space,
Between the light and shadow's grace.
Accept them both, let life expand,
Its harmony within your hand.

The Light Beyond

The shadows dance, they twist and play,
Yet light is never far away.
It pierces through the darkest shroud,
A gentle beam, a promise loud.
In sorrow's depths, the light is near,
A quiet glow to soothe the fear.
And in the light, the shadow hides,
A depth that strengthens, where truth abides.
No moment stays, no season lingers,
Yet balance rests within your fingers.
Hold both with care, let neither weigh,
For both will come, and both will stray.
The light beyond the shadow's flight,
Reveals the beauty of the night.

The Dual Path

The road divides, yet joins again,
Through hills of light, through shadowed glen.
Each turn reveals a different hue,
Yet both are paths that lead to you.
The joy you seek, the pain you bear,
Are threads within the same repair.
One lifts you high, one grounds you deep,
Together forming truths to keep.
The path is neither wrong nor right,
It shifts with shadow, bends with light.
To walk the way, accept the blend,
Of joy that greets and pain that mends.
For every step, both dark and bright,
Creates the journey toward the light.

The Shadow's Song

The shadow sings a softer tune,
It dances low beneath the moon.
Its voice, though quiet, holds a tone,
That echoes truths we've often known.
The light responds, a vibrant flare,
A harmony beyond compare.
Together bound, they share the stage,
A dance that spans both youth and age.
For life's a song of highs and lows,
A shifting rhythm as it flows.
To hear it all, to let it be,
Is where we find true harmony.
The shadow's song, the light's refrain,
Together weave life's sweet domain.

Between the Poles

The pendulum swings from side to side,
Through joy's embrace and sorrow's tide.
It never rests, it doesn't stay,
Yet balance meets it on the way.
For every high, a low must come,
A beating heart, a steady drum.
The poles of life are not apart,
But threads that weave a single heart.
To sway with grace, to shift with ease,
To honour both, the sun and breeze.
This is the dance, the flow, the art,
Of living fully, every part.
Between the poles, where balance lies,
We find the truth beneath the skies.

The Light in the Dark

The darkest hour holds a spark,
A glimmer faint within the dark.
It waits for you to lift your gaze,
To guide you through the shadowed maze.
The light within the dark is real,
A force that time cannot conceal.
It whispers hope, it calls your name,
A quiet, steady, endless flame.
And when the light becomes too strong,
The shadow cools, it rights the wrong.
Together they create the frame,
For all that shifts, for all that came.
The light in the dark, the dark in the light,
Together form life's purest sight.

The Eternal Exchange

The light will fade, the dark will rise,
A cycle endless as the skies.
Yet neither claims the final throne,
Each shares the stage, yet stands alone.
The day's bright rays will kiss the night,
The stars will hum a tune of light.
This ebb and flow, this constant trade,
The source from which all life is made.
No need to hold, no need to flee,
Both dark and light are meant to be.
Release the grip, let balance reign,
Both joy and sorrow must remain.
The eternal exchange of shadow and glow,
Teaches the path that all must know.

The Shadow's Embrace

The shadow bends, it holds you near,
A space of rest, a calm sincere.
It does not harm, it does not hate,
It simply holds the hand of fate.
The light will come, its warmth will stay,
Until the shadow claims its day.
Yet neither fights, they intertwine,
A dance of balance, so divine.
The shadow's embrace is not to fear,
It teaches strength, it draws you near.
For every dark contains a spark,
A guide that leads you through the arc.
In shadow's arms, the truth will show,
To find the light, let shadows grow.

The Endless Journey

The path winds on, it has no end,
Through fields of gold, through turns that bend.
Each step we take, a lesson taught,
Each pause we make, a mindful thought.
The road may twist, the skies may grey,
Yet still we walk, we find our way.
For every trial, for every cheer,
The journey calls, its truth is clear.
No need to rush, no need to fight,
The path unfolds in gentle light.
In every step, renewal grows,
The endless journey softly shows.

The Path Revealed

Beneath your feet, the path appears,
A winding way through hopes and fears.
Its stones may shift, its trail may fade,
Yet every step a mark is made.
The journey speaks in quiet tone,
It tells of all the soul has known.
Through mindful breath, through steady pace,
The path becomes a sacred space.
No need to see the journey's end,
Each step itself will guide and mend.
Through growth and stillness, joy and strife,
The path becomes the thread of life.

Steps in Time

Each step we take, a moment clear,
A quiet breath that draws us near.
The world expands, the heart takes root,
The journey flows in calm pursuit.
No race to run, no prize to find,
The path itself fulfils the mind.
Through mindful steps, the soul will see,
The gift of life's simplicity.
The road will stretch, the years will flow,
Yet with each step, the self will grow.
A path without an end or start,
Its map is written in the heart.

The Way of Being

The path we walk is not a line,
But circles drawn in time's design.
Each turn we take, a chance to grow,
Each pause we make, a truth to know.
The journey asks for nothing more,
Than presence with what lies in store.
No need to run, no need to race,
The path will lead to every place.
In every step, a moment waits,
A mindful key to open gates.
The way of being, vast and free,
The path is all we need to be.

Through the Seasons

The path we walk through every year,
Will shift with seasons bright and clear.
In spring, it blooms; in fall, it fades,
Yet still its beauty never sways.
Each step we take, a chapter new,
A thread of light in every hue.
Through summer's warmth, through winter's chill,
The path endures, it guides us still.
The journey flows, it bends, it blends,
A timeless road that never ends.
Through change and growth, the truth remains,
The mindful path forever gains.

The Traveler's Way

The traveller knows the path is long,
Its rhythm beats, a quiet song.
No map to hold, no guide to lead,
The path unfolds with every deed.
Through every turn, through every mile,
The journey's gift—a fleeting smile.
Each mindful step becomes the guide,
As moments teach and fears subside.
The traveller walks, not to arrive,
But simply to feel alive.
The path without an end will show,
The way to learn, the way to grow.

A Timeless Trail

The path extends beyond the sight,
It glows in day, it whispers night.
Its twists and turns, its rise and fall,
A mirror for the self in all.
Each step is sacred, small yet vast,
A journey rooted in the past.
Yet with each breath, the path renews,
A canvas fresh in endless hues.
The trail will never end its call,
For growth and peace embrace us all.
The mindful walk, a steady flame,
A timeless trail, both wild and tame.

The Infinite Road

The road ahead holds countless bends,
A way that weaves, that never ends.
Through shadows deep, through sunlit streams,
The path becomes a place of dreams.
No end to seek, no goal to find,
The journey rests within the mind.
Each step we take, a present gift,
A mindful pause, a gentle shift.
The infinite road will guide and show,
Through every rise, through every low.
With open heart, its truth we feel,
A path of life, a path of real.

General Advice for Mantra Practice

Create a Ritual: Dedicate a few minutes daily to repeating your chosen mantra, either silently or aloud. Morning or evening works well, but anytime you feel distracted or need focus can be beneficial.

Pair with Breathwork: As you repeat a mantra, synchronize it with your breathing. For example, inhale while silently saying the first half of the mantra and exhale while finishing it.

Write It Down: Keep your mantras visible by writing them on sticky notes, setting them as phone reminders, or journaling about them. Seeing the words can reinforce their impact.

Meditate with Mantras: Sit in stillness, close your eyes, and repeat your mantra as a meditation focus. This practice helps deepen its influence and allows it to permeate your subconscious mind.

Embody the Words: Reflect on actions that align with your mantra. For instance, if your mantra is about renewal, consider taking a restorative walk, drinking water mindfully, or clearing out mental or physical clutter.

Be Patient with Yourself: Growth and renewal take time. Trust that consistent practice with these mantras will help create a steady, lasting shift in your mindset and life.

By integrating these mantras and practices into your daily routine, you can cultivate a life of continuous growth, mindfulness, and renewal.

Mantra 1: "I release what no longer serves me to make space for growth."

Advice: Reflect on aspects of your life—habits, beliefs, or relationships—that may be holding you back. Use this mantra during moments of letting go, such as decluttering your space, journaling, or meditating. Visualization can be a powerful tool: imagine releasing old energy and welcoming new, vibrant energy.

Mantra 2: "I embrace each step of my journey with curiosity and grace."

Advice: Life is not about rushing to the finish line; it's about being present with each step. Repeat this mantra when you feel impatient or discouraged. Pair it with mindful walking or breathing exercises to reconnect with the moment.

Mantra 3: "Growth begins in stillness; I honour my need for rest and renewal."

Advice: Recognize that growth often requires pauses for reflection and rest. Use this mantra during self-care routines, such as taking a bath, practicing yoga, or simply sitting quietly in nature. It reminds you that rest is not weakness but a vital part of renewal.

Mantra 4: "I have the courage to evolve and the patience to unfold."

Advice: Growth is a process, not an instant transformation. Use this mantra when you feel overwhelmed by the challenges of personal growth. Combine it with deep breathing to calm your mind and reassure yourself that progress is happening, even if it's not immediately visible.

Mantra 5: "I nurture the seeds of change within me."

Advice: Every small action contributes to your growth. This mantra can accompany intentional acts like journaling about your goals, planting actual seeds in a garden, or setting daily intentions. It reminds you that small efforts compound into significant transformations.

Mantra 6: "I am grounded in my strength and open to renewal."

Advice: Growth requires balance between being grounded and embracing change. Use this mantra when you feel unsteady, such as during transitions or moments of doubt. Pair it with grounding exercises like standing barefoot on the earth or visualizing roots extending from your feet into the ground.

Mantra 7: "Every breath I take is an opportunity to begin again."

Advice: Life offers endless chances to reset and start fresh. Repeat this mantra when you feel stuck or frustrated, especially during mindful breathing exercises. It reminds you that renewal is always accessible, no matter where you are in your journey.

Mantra 8: "I trust the process of growth, even when I cannot see the outcome."

Advice: Growth often feels unclear or slow. This mantra encourages trust in the unseen. Use it during uncertain times, repeating it while meditating or journaling to reinforce faith in your efforts and the journey ahead.

Mantra 9: "I align with my purpose and take steps toward my highest self."

Advice: This mantra helps refocus your energy on purposeful action. Use it at the start of your day or before making decisions. Pair it with goal-setting exercises or visualizations of your ideal self to anchor your actions in alignment with your values.

Mantra 10: "I honour my journey and celebrate my progress, no matter how small."

Advice: Growth is not linear, and every step forward is worth celebrating. Use this mantra during moments of reflection, such as before bed or after completing a task. Writing down small victories or expressing gratitude can help reinforce this practice.

Affirmations to Help Refocus, Develop Inner Growth, and Renewal

Affirmations are powerful tools for reprogramming the mind, fostering positive self-talk, and aligning your thoughts with your intentions. Below are affirmations to support your journey toward inner growth and renewal, along with practical advice on how to use them effectively.

How to Use Affirmations Effectively

Affirmations work best when they are used consistently and with intention. Here's how you can incorporate them into your daily life:

1. Set Aside Quiet Time

Choose a moment in your day—morning, evening, or during a break—when you can focus on your affirmations without distraction.

Sit comfortably, take a few deep breaths, and center your thoughts.

2. Speak Them Aloud or Silently

Repeat your chosen affirmation aloud, allowing yourself to hear and feel the words, or say it silently with focused intention. Speaking aloud can create a stronger emotional connection.

3. Write Them Down

Write your affirmations in a journal, notebook, or on sticky notes that you place around your home or workspace. Seeing them throughout the day reinforces their impact.

4. Pair with Visualizations

As you repeat an affirmation, visualize it as if it's already true. For instance, imagine yourself confidently navigating a challenge or feeling calm and renewed after letting go of stress.

5. Integrate with Daily Activities

Use affirmations during routine tasks, such as brushing your teeth or commuting. Linking them to habitual activities helps make them a natural part of your day.

6. Practice Gratitude

Combine affirmations with gratitude by acknowledging what you're thankful for as you affirm your intentions. Gratitude amplifies the positive energy of affirmations.

7. Create a Ritual

Start or end your day with affirmations to set the tone or reflect on your progress. Light a candle, play calming music, or practice deep breathing to enhance the experience.

8. Stay Consistent

Use your affirmations daily. Consistency helps rewire thought patterns, making them an integral part of your mindset.

9. Modify as Needed

Tailor affirmations to suit your specific goals or challenges. For example, if you're facing a stressful period, focus on affirmations that promote calm and resilience.

10. Pair with Physical Movement

Combine affirmations with yoga, walking, or stretching. This helps integrate the affirmations into your body and reinforces a sense of alignment.

Advice for Maximizing Affirmation Practice

Start with Belief: Choose affirmations that resonate with you and feel achievable. If an affirmation feels too distant from your current mindset, modify it to feel more authentic. For example, instead of "I am completely at peace," you might say, "I am learning to find peace within myself."

Focus on the Present: Frame affirmations in the present tense. This reinforces the idea that growth and renewal are already in motion.

Be Patient: The effects of affirmations are cumulative. Trust that with consistent practice, your mindset will shift, and positive changes will manifest.

Use Emotion: Speak or think affirmations with feeling. Engage your heart as well as your mind to deepen their impact.

Track Progress: Reflect on how affirmations influence your thoughts and actions over time. Journaling about your experiences can help you see your growth.

Sample Daily Affirmation Practice

Morning Ritual:

Begin your day with 5 minutes of affirmations, such as:

"I approach today with an open heart and a clear mind."

"I am capable of handling whatever comes my way."

Say these affirmations in front of a mirror for added confidence.

Midday Refocus:

During a break, take 2-3 minutes to repeat affirmations silently or aloud, such as:

"I release stress and invite calm into my life."

"Every breath renews my energy and focus."

Evening Reflection:

Reflect on the day with affirmations like:

"I am proud of the progress I made today."

"I let go of what I cannot control and rest with ease."

By using these affirmations and techniques, you can cultivate a mindset of continuous growth and renewal. Affirmations act as gentle reminders of your resilience, self-worth, and capacity for transformation, empowering you to navigate life's journey with mindfulness and grace.

Affirmations for Inner Growth and Renewal

"I release the past and embrace the present moment."

Let go of regrets and what no longer serves you. Focus on the opportunities each new moment brings.

"I am capable of growth, even through challenges."

Remind yourself that struggles are stepping stones toward strength and wisdom.

"I am open to change and trust the process of transformation."

Embrace the flow of life, understanding that change is essential for personal renewal.

"Every day, I take one step closer to becoming my best self."

Focus on consistent, small actions that contribute to lasting growth.

"I am resilient, and I rise above obstacles with grace."

Build confidence in your ability to navigate challenges and thrive.

"I honour my journey and celebrate my progress."

Acknowledge how far you've come, even if the steps feel small.

"I am grounded, calm, and connected to my inner strength."

Reinforce a sense of stability and self-trust during stressful times.

"I deserve rest, reflection, and renewal."

Give yourself permission to slow down and recharge without guilt.

"I am grateful for every opportunity to grow and evolve."

Cultivate gratitude as a foundation for embracing growth.

"I trust myself to make choices that align with my values and purpose."

Strengthen your confidence in your ability to make decisions that honour your path.

Disclaimer

The content within this book is intended for informational and inspirational purposes only. While the practices, poems, affirmations, and techniques shared here aim to promote mindfulness, self-awareness, and inner peace, they are not a substitute for professional advice, therapy, or medical treatment.

Readers are encouraged to approach the suggested exercises and reflections with mindfulness and self-compassion, adapting them to their individual needs and circumstances. If you have a medical condition, mental health concern, or are experiencing significant distress, please consult with a qualified healthcare or mental health professional.

The author and publisher disclaim any liability arising directly or indirectly from the use of this book. The journey of growth and mindfulness is deeply personal, and readers are invited to engage with the material at their own pace and discretion.

By embracing these reflections and practices, you take the first step toward a more mindful and fulfilling life. Thank you for allowing this book to be part of your journey.

Milton Keynes UK
Ingram Content Group UK Ltd.
UKHW030823181124
451360UK00001B/196